DATE DUE

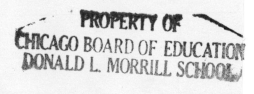

Renewable Energy

Jacqueline Dineen

RSVP

RAINTREE
STECK-VAUGHN
P U B L I S H E R S
The Steck-Vaughn Company

Austin, Texas

Editor: Claire Llewellyn
Science Editor: Kim Merlino
Design: Carolyn Ginesi
Project Manager: Julie Klaus
Electronic Production: Scott Melcer
Artwork: Raymond Turvey
Cover Art: Raymond Turvey
Picture Research: Alison Renwick

Library of Congress
Cataloging-in-Publication Data
Dineen, Jacqueline..
    Renewable Energy/Jacqueline
    Dineen.
        p.   cm. — (What about?)
    Includes index.
    ISBN 0-8114-5524-6
    1. Renewable energy sources—
Juvenile literature. [1. Renewable
energy sources. 2. Power
resources.]   I. Title.   II. Series.
TJ808.2.D57 1995
621.042—dc20   94-30548
                                 CIP
                                 AC
Printed and bound in the
United States by Lake Book,
Melrose Park, IL

1 2 3 4 5 6 7 8 9 0 LB 98 97 96 95

Contents

New Forms of Energy

Most electricity is produced by burning coal, oil, or natural gas. The heat is used to boil water to make steam, which drives machinery. Coal, oil, and natural gas are **fossil fuels**, and they will be all used up one day. We need to find other ways of producing electricity. There are other **energy** sources, such as the sun, wind, and moving water.

▽ Power plants use fossil fuels, like coal, at a shocking rate. Fossil fuels, which took millions of years to form, may have disappeared within 100 years.

Sources of Renewable Energy

The sun, the wind, and flowing water are **renewable energy sources** that will never run out. The sun's energy can be used to make electricity. The energy of moving water and wind can drive machinery. Underground rocks provide heat called geothermal energy. The problem with these sources is that they may not provide energy when we want or need it.

▽ Everyone has felt the energy of the sun. Its energy can be stored to provide heat in the home. It can also be changed into electricity.

We enjoy and put the power of the wind to use. But the wind does not always blow when we want it to.

5

Solar Power

Solar power means "power from the sun." A simple way to use solar power is to trap sunlight to heat a greenhouse. Solar panels are now used to collect sunlight and store the energy for heating. Solar **cells** "change" sunlight into electricity. They are used on very different kinds of equipment, such as **satellites** and pocket calculators!

▷ Solar power provides the electricity needed by satellites as they circle the Earth.

▽ Solar cells provide enough energy to keep these street lights on in Israel.

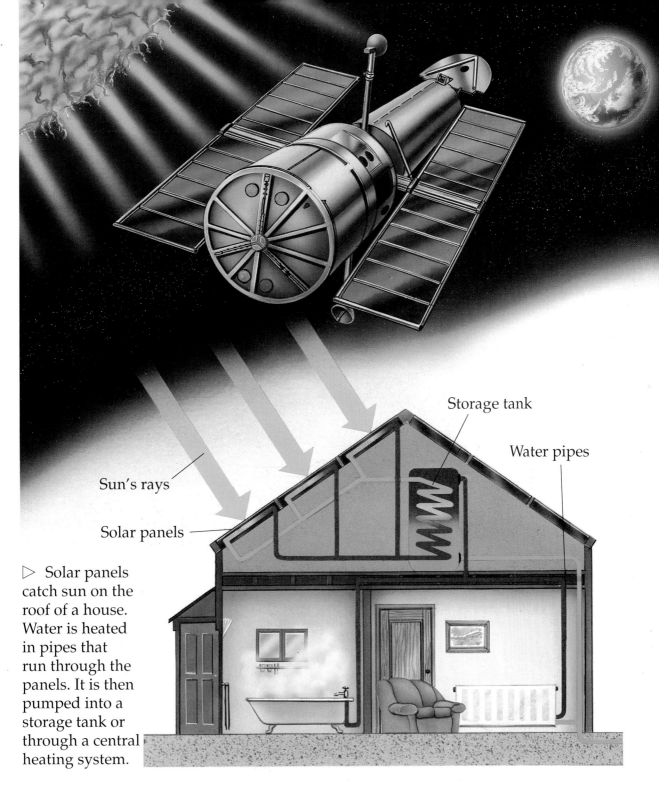

Storage tank

Water pipes

Sun's rays

Solar panels

▷ Solar panels
catch sun on the
roof of a house.
Water is heated
in pipes that
run through the
panels. It is then
pumped into a
storage tank or
through a central
heating system.

A Solar Power Plant

At a solar power plant, huge mirrors are positioned to catch the sun as it moves across the sky. The sunlight is reflected onto a boiler. A large amount of heat builds up and turns the water in the boiler into steam. The steam drives a machine called a **generator**, which produces electricity.

▷ A solar power plant in Albuquerque, New Mexico.

▽ A solar power plant turns the sun's energy into useful electricity.

The sun's rays strike the mirrors.

The rays are reflected onto a boiler.

The water boils and produces steam.

The steam turns the generator.

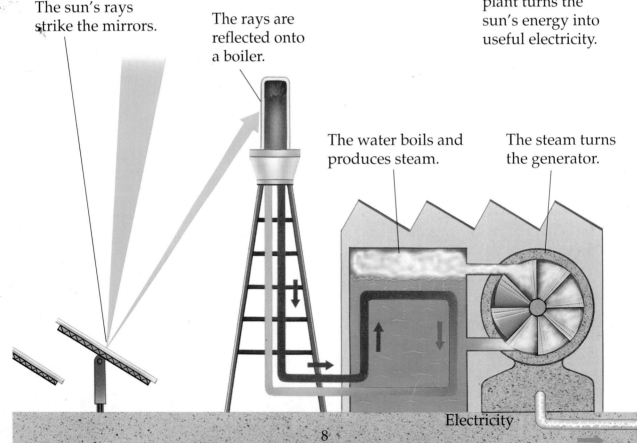

Electricity

Wind Power

People have used the power of the wind for centuries. Sailors learned that wind blowing against the sail of a ship would push it through the water. By about 1150, people in Europe were using windmills to pump water and grind grain. As the wind turns the sails of a windmill, the sails turn an iron bar that drives machinery inside the mill.

▽ Windmills are still used to pump flood water from low-lying land in the Netherlands. The canal carries the water away.

▷ This windmill is used to grind grain. The turning sails (or blades) move a pole called a shaft. Machinery inside the mill turns the millstone, which grinds the grain into flour.

Sail

Shaft

Grain

Millstone

Flour

On a Wind Farm

A wind **turbine** is a machine that uses the power of the wind to produce electricity. It is based on the same principle as the windmill, although it looks very different. The turbine has two or three blades and a tail vane to keep it turned into the wind. One turbine cannot produce much electricity. A wind farm is a group of turbines operating together.

▷ The spinning blades of the turbine turn a shaft inside the cabin. The shaft drives a generator that produces electricity.

▽ Wind farms are built in places where there is always plenty of wind, such as on cliffs and hilltops.

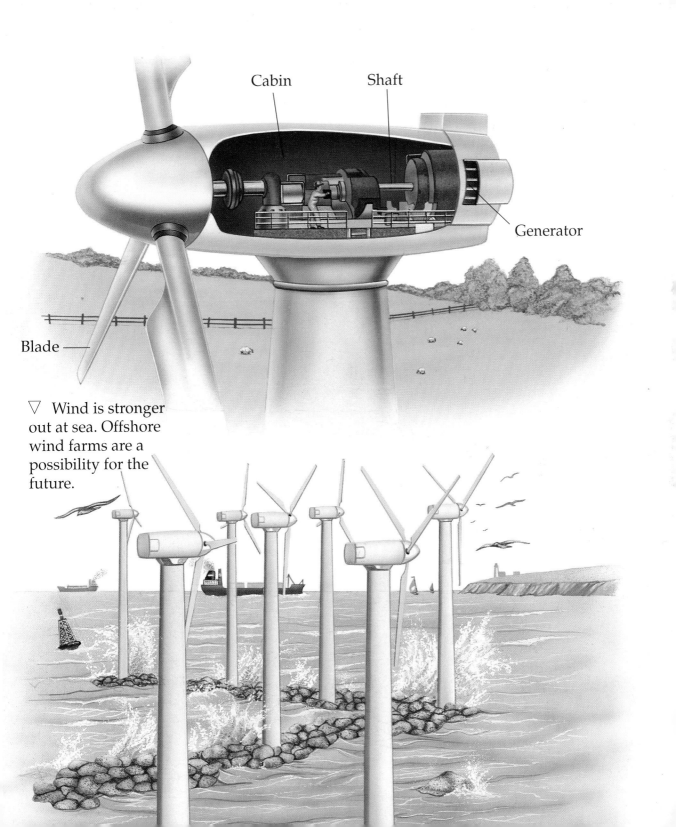

Cabin

Shaft

Generator

Blade

▽ Wind is stronger out at sea. Offshore wind farms are a possibility for the future.

Water Power

A fast-flowing river has a lot of energy. People have been using water power to drive waterwheels for about 2,000 years. The waterwheels were connected to machinery that turned millstones for grinding grain. Waterwheels were also used to drive machinery in cloth mills and other factories.

▷ Water mills were built on the banks of rivers.

◁ There are two types of waterwheels. In the undershot wheel, the lower blades of the wheel are under the water. The flow of water pushes them around.

▷ In the overshot wheel, the water flows along a chute. It drops on to one paddle after another and turns the wheel around.

14

Hydroelectric Power

Rushing water can be used to turn turbines and to produce electricity. The water has to flow with great force. At a **hydroelectric** power plant, a supply of water is stored behind a dam until a **reservoir** is formed. When the gates of the dam are opened, a powerful rush of water surges through huge tunnels and turns the turbines.

▷ When the gates in the dam are opened, water thunders down the tunnels and makes the turbines spin. The turbines drive generators that produce electricity.

▽ Hydroelectric power plants are constructed in the mountains where dams can be built.

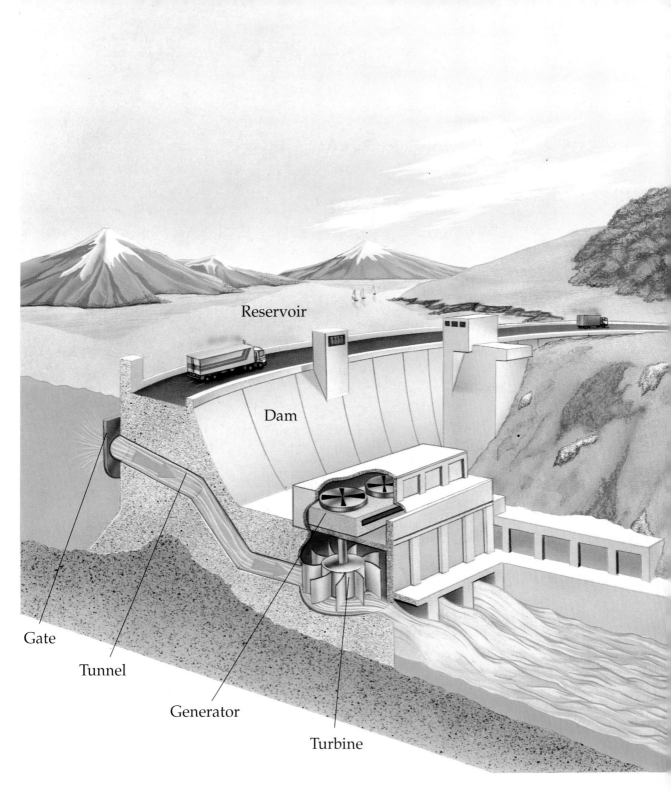

Reservoir

Dam

Gate

Tunnel

Generator

Turbine

Tidal Power

High and low tides in the ocean are caused by the pull of **gravity**, mainly from the moon. Unlike other sources of renewable energy, we can count on the tides. They have been used to drive water mills for hundreds of years. Water is trapped in a pond at high tide, and then let out when the tide has gone out. As it rushes out, the water turns a mill wheel.

▷ A very old tidal mill in Essex.

▽ As the moon moves around the Earth, its gravity pulls on the Earth.

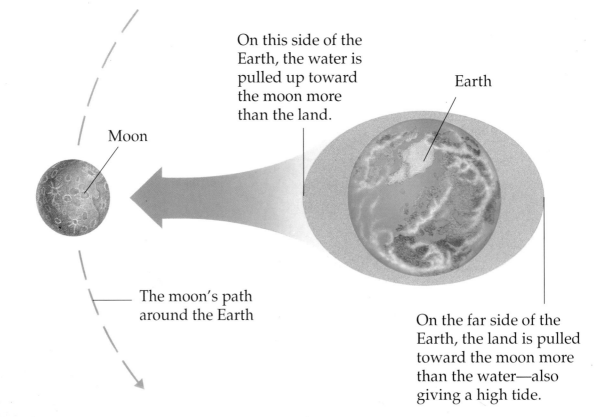

On this side of the Earth, the water is pulled up toward the moon more than the land.

Earth

Moon

The moon's path around the Earth

On the far side of the Earth, the land is pulled toward the moon more than the water—also giving a high tide.

A Tidal Power Plant

Tidal power plants are built in places where there is a big difference between high and low tide. For example, in the Bay of Fundy in Canada the water rises about 49 feet (15 m) at high tide. Tidal power plants use the same method as tidal mills. Water rushes to a lower level and turns a turbine as it rushes through. The turbine drives a generator.

▷ At high tide, water surges up through the open gates, turning the turbines. The gates close to trap the water.

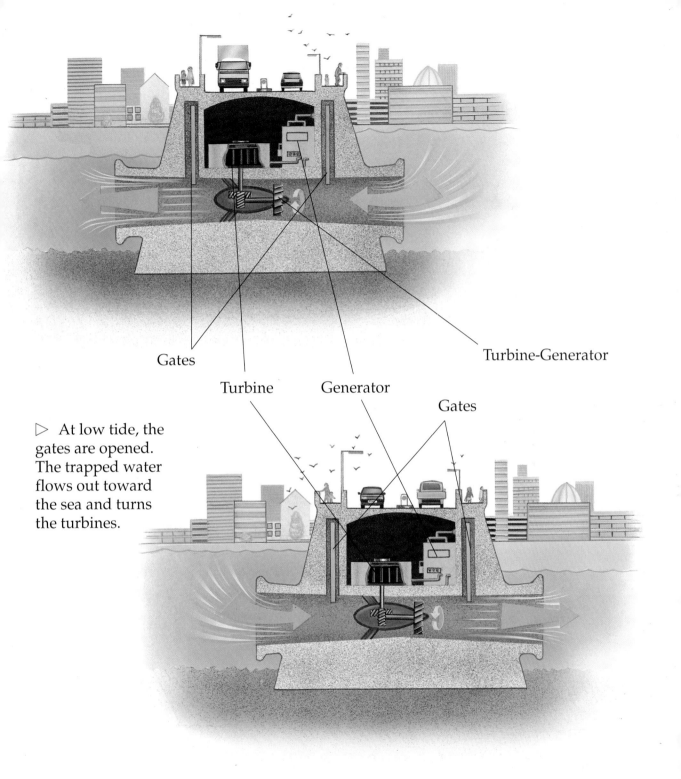

Gates

Turbine-Generator

Turbine   Generator

Gates

▷ At low tide, the gates are opened. The trapped water flows out toward the sea and turns the turbines.

21

Wave Energy

Waves are a very powerful source of renewable energy. They are caused by the wind blowing across wide stretches of water far out in the ocean. Waves reach the coast. They batter the shore and **erode** the rocks and cliffs. If this energy were controlled, it could be used to produce electricity.

▷ Waves are most powerful during a storm. They crash onto the beach with great force.

▽ Ocean waves are so powerful that they can toss boats and huge tree trunks up onto the shore.

Controlling the Waves

Scientists are testing several different wave machines. They all use the up-and-down motion of waves to turn a turbine and produce electricity. The best-known machine is the Salter Ducks. It has a row of floats that bob up and down on the waves. As they move, they pump powerful jets of water along a pipe that turns the blades of a turbine.

▷ This wave machine, called the "Clam," uses the rise and fall of the waves to move air over a turbine.

▽ The Salter Ducks. As the floats bob up and down, their energy will be used to create electricity.

▽ Cockerell's Rafts are another kind of wave machine. As the rafts move, they pump air that turns a turbine.

Geothermal Energy

Heat is trapped in rocks deep in the Earth. This is known as geothermal energy. If water collects near these hot rocks, it heats up and may shoot back to the surface. It comes out as a hot water spring or as steam. This hot water or steam can be piped to a geothermal power plant where it drives a generator.

▷ This hot spring, or geyser, is in New Zealand.

▽ The rainwater has seeped down through soft rock. It may collect above a layer of hot hard rock. Then it may shoot up as steam or as a hot spring.

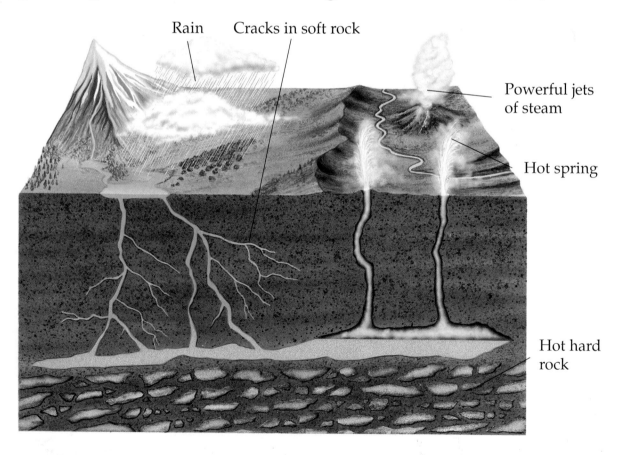

Rain

Cracks in soft rock

Powerful jets of steam

Hot spring

Hot hard rock

A Geothermal Power Plant

A geothermal power plant makes use of underground heat to produce electricity. Two pipelines are drilled down to hot underground rocks. Water is pumped down one pipe and changed into steam by the hot rocks. The steam shoots up a second pipe, driving the turbines in the power plant above.

▽ Geothermal power plants are rare. They have been built in the United States, Iceland, New Zealand, Australia, and Japan.

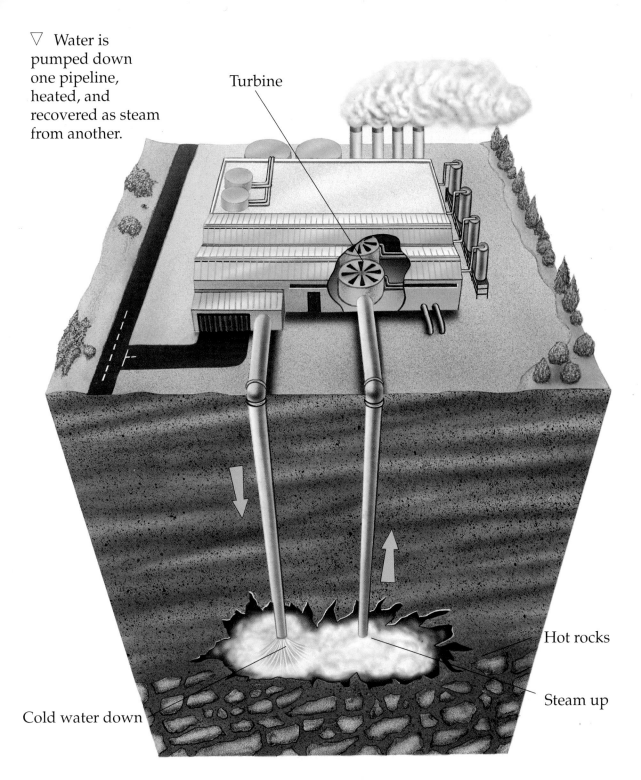

▽ Water is pumped down one pipeline, heated, and recovered as steam from another.

Turbine

Hot rocks

Steam up

Cold water down

29

Things to Do

- Did you know that bananas grow in Iceland? Find out how they are grown and which kind of energy is used.

- Design a solar-powered house. Which way should your house face to catch the most sunlight?

- Think of a good place to build a wind farm. Is there a suitable place near where you live?

Useful Addresses:

U.S. Department of Energy
Conservation and Renewable
  Energy
1000 Independence Ave., S.W.
Washington, DC 20585
(202) 586-9220

Worldwatch Institute
1776 Massachusetts Ave., N.W.
Washington, DC 20036
(202) 452-1999

Conservation and Renewable
  Energy
Inquiry and Referral Service
P.O. Box 8900
Silver Spring, MD 20907
(800) 523-2929

Alliance to Save Energy
1725 K Street, N.W., Suite 509
Washington, DC 20006-1401
(202) 857-0666

Glossary

atmosphere   The layer of gases that surrounds the Earth.

cell   A small unit for making electricity. A battery is a cell.

energy   The power to do work and drive machines.

erode   To wear away by wind or moving water.

fossil fuel   A fuel made from the remains of animals and plants that died millions of years ago. Oil, gas, and coal are fossil fuels.

generator   A machine for producing electricity.

gravity   The natural force that pulls all things together, such as the force between the moon and the Earth.

hydroelectric   Producing electricity by the power of falling water.

renewable energy sources   Energy sources that do not get used up. Water and wind are renewable energy sources.

reservoir   A place where a large amount of water is stored.

satellite   A human-made object that circles the Earth to take pictures or send signals.

turbine   The part of a generator or any engine that is made to turn by the force of pressure.

Index

Photographic Credits:
J. Allan Cash 6, 14, 20; Martin Bond/Environmental
Picture Library 3, 19; Martin Bond/Science Photo
Library 25; Robert Harding Picture Library 10, 12, 23,
28; J. Holmes/Environmental Picture Library 4; C.
Jones/Environmental Picture Library 27; John
Mead/Science Photo Library 16; Peter
Menzel/Science Photo Library 9.